THE STONES OF
· THE TEMPLE ·

To Vicki
—JFV

To Steve
—KBP

Deseret Book is a registered trademark of Deseret Book Company.
Printed in Hong Kong.

10 9 8 7 6 5 4 3 2 1

ISBN 0-87579-735-0

Designed by Richard Erickson and Pat Bagley.
Illustrations were done with pastels on textured mat board.
Text was set in Novarese.

THE STONES OF
· THE TEMPLE ·

Written by

J. Frederic Voros, Jr.

Illustrated by

Kathleen B. Peterson

DESERET BOOK COMPANY
AND PRIMARY PRESS
SALT LAKE CITY, UTAH

Brother Brigham struck his cane upon the ground. "Here we shall build a temple to our God," he said. He saw in vision a temple with six towers. And the work began.

Mormon men pulled granite from the walls of Little Cottonwood Canyon, twenty miles south and east of Temple Square. Granite cold and hard, formed in the earth, stone made of other stones: feldspar, quartz, and mica. From the quarries of the canyon came the stones of the temple.

Quarrymen broke the stones into blocks. They hammered spikes in a line into the granite stones, striking sparks, cracking and breaking the huge rocks, making them into the stones of the temple.

Stones split and squared, rough cut, were hauled
by wagons down the canyon to the Temple Block.
Oxen labored, heads bowed, blowing steamy
breath, pulling the stones of the temple.

One hundred feet wide, nearly two hundred long, the foundation of the temple was laid. Stones long and deep, crosswise and upright: maze of stones. In the sunlight laughing children played in the maze, hide-and-seek among the stones of the temple.

Year by year, for forty years, the temple rose: walls nine feet thick at the base, soaring towers topped with parapets, stately spires—all grew stone by stone amid scaffolding and derricks.

Then, on April 6th, 1893, Wilford Woodruff, white-haired prophet stooped with age, bowed his head and prayed and gave the house to God. And the people shouted, "Hosanna! Hosanna to God and the Lamb!"

Look at the temple: its walls and towers and windows tell of heaven. There are sun stones and star stones and stones with the moon in phases. Window casings are carved with clasping hands and the all-seeing eye of God. On the west face is the Big Dipper pointing to the North Star, our Guide.

Atop the capstone stands a figure made of hammered copper covered with gold. Book-bringer, herald of dawn, bright angel Moroni lifts his trumpet to the ear of God.

Within the doors and walls, within the temple, is a font where the living are baptized for the dead. It rests upon the backs of twelve oxen of cast iron and bronze, oxen like the ones that hauled stones from the canyon.

There too are mirrors, altars, windows of stained glass, and silken curtains. Through the mirrors and altars, through the windows and curtains, saints seek after One greater than the temple.

Six towers, three and three, each with twelve spires around a central spire; and every spire like a prayer offered up by the quarrymen, the straining oxen, the laughing children, the golden trumpeter, the white-haired prophet—prayers offered up to where God lives and hears and looks down upon the temple.

It is His house. The walls are His; the towers and spires are His; the doors and windows, the sun, the moon, and the stars, the clasping hands—all are His; the altars are His; the quarrymen, the straining oxen, the laughing children, the golden trumpeter, the praying prophet and the shouting people—all these are His; and you too are His.

The temple will stand a thousand years. But you are His forever, like the children laughing in the sunlight, playing hide-and-seek among the stones of the temple.

NOTES ON ILLUSTRATIONS

BRIGHAM YOUNG AND THE TEMPLE: Brigham Young designated the temple site on July 28, 1847.

LITTLE COTTONWOOD CANYON: Oolite from Sanpete Valley, sandstone from Redbutte Canyon, and adobe were considered for building material before deciding on granite.

TOOLS: Single jackhammer, finishing drill, and facing chisel.

SPLITTING BLOCKS: To split the boulders, one man would swing the sledgehammer while another man would hold and turn the drill. The holes were drilled three-and-a-half inches deep four to seven inches apart. A wedge was inserted into each hole and then tapped until the boulder split.

HAULING BLOCKS: The stones weighed from two to six thousand pounds each, and the round trip from quarry to Temple Block and back took four days.

STONES ON TEMPLE BLOCK: The buildings in the background are the Tabernacle on the left and the Endowment House on the right.

SCAFFOLDING ON THE TEMPLE: Truman O. Angell, Sr., was the temple architect. At his death in 1887, his son, Truman, Jr., replaced him, and later, Joseph Don Carlos Young became the architect.

HOSANNA SHOUT: Over fifty thousand people attended the outdoor capstone-laying ceremony in April 1892. After giving the shout, they sang "The Spirit of God Like a Fire Is Burning."

WILFORD WOODRUFF: After President Woodruff offered thanks and dedicated and consecrated the temple, the hosanna shout was given three times, the choir sang, and Elder Lorenzo Snow offered the benediction. Because the temple could hold only 2150 people, the service was repeated numerous times until more than eighty-two thousand people had attended.

EAST FACE OF THE TEMPLE: The center tower rises 210 feet. In descending order on the tower are the angel Moroni, cloud stones, the dedicatory inscription (which begins "Holiness to the Lord/The House of the Lord"), the all-seeing eye, the alpha omega inscription, and the clasped hands. All the towers also feature star, sun, moon, and earth stones.

ANGEL MORONI: Cyrus Dallin sculpted the statue, which stands 12 feet 5 1/2 inches tall and weighs fifteen hundred pounds. It is made of copper covered with gold leaf.

BAPTISMAL FONT: The basin, which holds nearly five hundred gallons of water, rests on the back of twelve oxen representing the twelve tribes of Israel.

ALTAR: The West Sealing Room on the third floor of the temple, featuring a stained glass depiction of Moroni delivering the Book of Mormon plates to Joseph Smith.

SIX TOWERS: The three towers on the east are higher than those on the west. The east towers represent the Melchizedek Priesthood and the President of the Church with his two counselors, and the west towers represent the Aaronic Priesthood and the Presiding Bishop and his two counselors.

WEST FACE OF TEMPLE: The center tower rises 204 feet. In descending order on the tower are the cloud stones, the Big Dipper, the all-seeing eye, and the clasped hands.

SIDE VIEW OF TEMPLE: View of the temple from the south. The side rises 167 feet 6 inches. There are fifty moon stones that encircle the temple, each showing a different phase of the moon during the year.